Samuel H. Kellogg

From Death to Ressurrection

Samuel H. Kellogg

From Death to Ressurrection

ISBN/EAN: 9783337404444

Printed in Europe, USA, Canada, Australia, Japan

Cover: Foto ©Lupo / pixelio.de

More available books at **www.hansebooks.com**

FROM

DEATH TO RESURRECTION;

OR,

SCRIPTURE TESTIMONY CONCERNING THE SAINTED DEAD.

BY

S. H. KELLOGG, D.D.,

Professor in the Western Theological Seminary, Allegheny, Pa.

AUTHOR OF

" *The Jews,*" "*The Light of Asia and the Light of the World,*" *etc.*

CONTENTS.

FROM DEATH TO RESURRECTION.

THE QUESTION.

UCH has been written, especially of late years, upon the state of the soul after death. It is not strange. Few questions are of more practical, personal interest than this. For until the generation which shall witness the personal advent of the Lord, among whom, we are told in Holy Scripture, there shall be some who "shall not sleep,"* we all have sooner or later to face the mystery of death. That day can not be far away from any of us at the furthest; it may, to any of us, be very near.

And even before we are called to solve the mystery by our personal experience, we are made from time to time to face it in the experience of others. Again and again we are called to stand beside the bedside of the dying.

---

* I Cor. xv. 51 ; 2 Thess. iv. 17.

With swelling heart we have watched the
changing face, and listened in anguish to the
shortening breath; we have spoken or looked
the last good-bye, and then, in an instant, the
departing one has passed out of sight and out
of hearing, into the world of the unknown!

There lies the body, but yesterday, perhaps,
so full of life and animation, and now an in-
sensate piece of clay! A moment ago, and
he we loved was here; and now, in one moment, that which was speaking to us, that
which we loved and which loved us, is gone!
gone!—and so very far, far away! How the
thoughts rush in upon the mind at such a
time! what great soul-possessing questions
tumultuously throng up in such an hour for
answer! But an answer neither experience
nor reason have to give.

Yet, where experience is silent and reason
bewildered, fancy and imagination have had
much to say. From time to time are offered
us new theories which set forth, with whatsoever plausibility or lack of plausibility, the
speculations of their several authors as to the
life of the disembodied soul. To recapitulate
these theories here is needless. They may for

the time beguile the heart of some, but they can none of them give satisfaction to any one who seeks for certitude of knowledge in this matter. One man's dreams and speculations here are as good as another's. We may well leave these eschatologies of the imagination to refute each other.

But there is one source from which we may hope for light upon this subject. Though experience and reason can tell us nothing, and fancy and imagination only mock us with ever-dissolving phantasies, we may turn hopefully to the Word of the ever-living God. The men who spake "the wisdom of God,"* "as they were moved by the Holy Ghost," † can be trusted to help us here. For they spake from Christ, and it is He, He only, who died and lived again, whose are "the keys of death and of Hades," ‡ that can tell us, as "the Amen, the faithful and true Witness," § how it is with those who have passed behind the veil. To Him and to His inspired Word we come with these questionings of our souls.

---

* 1 Cor. ii. 7.   † 2 Pet. i. 21.   ‡ Rev. i. 18.
§ Rev. iii. 14.

What does that Word teach us as to the state upon which believers enter at death?

NOT A FINAL STATE.

WE answer, in the first place, Holy Scripture teaches that the believer does *not* yet at death enter on his *final* state. Not yet even has he fully apprehended that for which he was apprehended of Christ Jesus. Let us mark and emphasize this well, that the Word of God does not teach that he who dies in Christ has yet attained his final state. He has reached, as we shall see, a blessed state; it is "far better" with him than it was here;* but for all that, it is not yet his final state. Better still is before him. Let us heed this the more carefully because here at once we find ourselves in opposition to the fancies of many, as to not a little of current theology. And yet whatsoever the opinions of men may be on the subject, if anything in the Scripture is clear, it is this, that although in the state of the righteous after death, there is

---

* Phil. i. 23.

much which is eternal, still the disembodied life upon which then they enter, is not, as such, eternal. Like this present life, it will at last have an end; but it will end, not by a death, but with re-embodiment, with resurrection.

This is plain from what the Word of God teaches concerning the resurrection of the dead. Sadly, alas, have many fallen away from the teachings of the Scripture and the hope of the primitive church concerning the resurrection of the dead. Many there are who tell us that by the resurrection of the dead is only meant the emancipation of the soul from the material embodiment in death. Others, again, dream of a so-called "spiritual" body—not that of which Paul tells us,* but that of Swedenborg;—a body which we are supposed to carry about with us, even now, and which being set free from this grosser body in the article of death, we have therein "the resurrection of the dead!"

But neither the one nor the other theory is the doctrine of the resurrection as we find

---

* 1 Cor. xv. 44.

it in the Holy Scripture. For they both alike identify death with resurrection, whereas the Scripture distinguishes and contrasts them. They make the resurrection in each case to be separate and merely individual, whereas the Scripture makes the resurrection of believers simultaneous.* They each make the resurrection to be a constantly occurring fact of the present age, whereas the Scripture makes the resurrection to be a fact of the future, the great event which ushers in what it calls "the age (or 'world') to come"; an event ordained to take place at the second coming of the Lord Jesus, "the Resurrection and the Life."† In a word, while these theorists hold to the word "resurrection," they deny the fact. For while the Bible teaches that it is that which died that rises, that which "is sown in corruption" which "is raised incorruptible,"‡ these teach that it is *not* that which dies that rises, but somewhat which never died at all, nor can die.

---

* I Cor. xv. 23; I Thess. iv. 13–18.

† John v. 28, 29; *et N. T. passim.*

‡ I Cor. xv. 36, 42.

We repeat, then, such theories as these, while pretending to affirm the truth, deny it outright.   If either of these too common views were the truth, then there were no resurrection of the dead ; and we were left, according to the logic of the inspired apostle, to face his awful conclusion : " If there be no resurrection of the dead, then is Christ not risen ; and if Christ is not risen, then is our preaching vain ; your faith is also vain ; ye are yet in your sins.   Then they also that are fallen asleep in Christ are perished." *

With a deep feeling of relief do we turn from these inane speculations of the modern children of Hymenæus and Philetus,† to the Word of God the Holy Ghost.   " We believe in the resurrection of the dead."   We find it written, " Them that sleep in Jesus shall God

---

* 1 Cor. xv. 14, 17, 18.

† " Shun profane and vain babblings ; for they will increase unto more ungodliness.   And their word will eat as doth a canker: of whom is Hymenæus and Philetus ; who concerning the truth have erred, saying that the resurrection is past already; and overthrow the faith of some."   2 Tim. ii. 16–18.

bring with Him."*   Not before that do they
rise.   For, again it is written, "We which are
alive and remain unto the coming of the Lord,
shall not precede them which are asleep. For
the Lord himself shall descend from heaven
with a shout, with the voice of the archangel,
and with the trump of God; and the dead in
Christ shall rise first; then we which are alive
and remain, shall be caught up together with
them in the clouds, to meet the Lord in the
air!"†   This is not a description of a death-
bed scene!   It announces something which
has never yet been seen; but which verily
shall be seen, in that day when the Crucified
One shall "appear the second time without
sin unto salvation."‡

But if there is to be a resurrection of the
dead,—if the soul of the departed saint is
again to assume, in the day of Christ's appearing, a bodily organization suited to its
glorified condition,—then it is certain that the
state into which the believer enters at death,
whatever else may be said of it, is not a final

---

* 1 Thess. iv. 14.   † *Ib*. vss. 15–17.
‡ Heb. ix. 28.

state. It is certain that it must be a condition profoundly contrasted, not only with the present life, but also with that upon which we shall enter with the future resurrection of the body.

The life of man therefore falls, not into two stages, as many are wont to speak, but into three. First, there is the stage from birth to death, which is a life in the "natural" or "animal"* body; second, the life from death to resurrection, which is life without a body; and third and final is the life from the resurrection on, which is life in the body spiritual and incorruptible.

MISAPPLIED SCRIPTURE.

WHEN we inquire more particularly what the Scriptures clearly teach as to the nature of this intermediate state—as we must rightly term it—we have to answer that they teach us surprisingly little. How little, in fact, they have to say about it, is the less realized by many that so frequently men have drawn

---

* 1 Cor. xv. 44. See Vulgate.

on the imagination to fill out a picture of which revelation has given but a bare outline. Still more often have men wrongly applied to the condition of believers in the intermediate state what the Scriptures only affirm of their condition after resurrection, thereby introducing a coloring into the picture of the disembodied life which does not belong there.

A familiar example of this misapplication of Scripture is furnished by the last two chapters of the Revelation of John. These are constantly cited as descriptive of the heaven into which we enter at death, while in point of fact, they contain no reference whatever thereto. So far is this from being true that among all the different systems of interpretation of this book, there is not one which makes these two chapters to be descriptive of the life between death and the resurrection. A very little examination of the plan of the Apocalypse, and especially of the context of these chapters, will make it clear to any one that such an application of them, however common it may be with the unthinking, and however endeared to us by long association, is wholly without warrant.

The vision of the Holy City, with its gates ·
of pearl and streets of gold, is made by the.
apostle to follow that of the judgment and the
great white throne. It is formally connected
with the latter by the words at the beginning
of chap. xxi., as setting forth a state of things
which follows chronologically upon the final
judgment. In the former vision, John had
seen the heavens and earth which now are,
pass away; in this vision, as succeeding
thereto, he tells us that he "saw a new heaven
and a new earth." Nor is the scene of the
vision the unseen world of spirits, or "heaven."
The place of the Holy City is the renewed
earth. We must not therefore go to these
chapters, as so many do, for information as
to the life of the believer immediately after
death. While certain statements therein made
are doubtless true also—as we learn from
other Scriptures—of believers even in the
intermediate state, they can not be quoted in
proof of any doctrine as to the disembodied
life before the resurrection. They are proof
passages for resurrection life, and for that
only.

In like manner, it may not be amiss to ob·

· serve, the common use of the phrase, "the
world to come," to denote the unseen spiritual world, or order of things, into which we
enter at death, is also without any warrant in
the Scripture. The phrase is no doubt a
Scriptural phrase, but this is not its Scriptural signification. In not a passage where it
is used in the New Testament, can it be shown
to have this meaning. Its sense must be his-
torically determined. We must understand the
phrase, not in any sense that may suit our
modern notions, but in that sense in which it
was used by the Jews to whom our Lord and
His apostles spoke and wrote. What that
sense was, is not a matter of dispute. The
phrase, "the world to come," (Greek, *ho aion
ho mellon;* Hebrew, *hà'olàm habbà*), was in-
variably used to denote, not the disembodied
state or the place of disembodied souls between death and the resurrection, but an
order of things on the earth, to be inherited,
as the Jews all believed, by the people of God
in the resurrection. The phrase were therefore better interpreted to our modern thought
by the words "the age to come." This is
suggested in the margin of the revised version,

in all places where this phrase occurs, with
one exception. That one exception is found
in Hebrews, ii. 5. In this passage, however,
the literal sense of the words rendered, "the
world to come," is as the margin of the revised version gives it, "*the inhabited earth* to
come." But this is further yet from any
possibility of application to the intermediate
state. No statement or suggestion which we
may find or think we find in passages in Scripture which speak of "the world to come"
can be quoted in proof of any doctrine with
regard to the intermediate state, either of the
saved or the lost. In every instance where the
words are used, they point us beyond the disembodied, to the re-embodied state in the
resurrection at Christ's second coming.

Illustrations of such misapplications of
Scripture to the intermediate state, need not
be further multiplied. When we have elim-
inated all conceptions of the disembodied life
which are derived from such misapplied Scripture, and all the conjectures of the imagination, we shall find that our residuum of positive
knowledge concerning the state of being in
which the Christian finds himself at death is

2

but small. Though it be little, however,—
far less than we could wish to know,—that
little is very definite and full of comfort.

A STATE OF CONSCIOUSNESS.

AS fundamental to all else, the Scriptures
teach that the intermediate state is a
state of consciousness.

It may indeed well be doubted whether the
words which our Lord quoted from the Old
Testament to the Sadducees,—" I am the God
of Abraham, the God of Isaac, and the God
of Jacob, etc."*—can be rightly adduced as
proof of this, as some have judged. For the
question with them was not as to the intermediate state, but as to the possibility of resurrection. This the Sadducees denied upon
materialistic grounds. As opposed to this
our Lord proves from the Pentateuch, which
they professed to believe, that Abraham and
the patriarchs were still alive. " God," was
His conclusion, " is not the God of the dead,
but of the living." But if alive, then the

---

* See Matt. xxii. 23–32.

Sadducees were wrong in denying the existence of spirit, and resurrection of the dead
was possible. But this only proves *life* in
the intermediate state, not *conscious* life. The
one does not involve the other.

But though we have not proof of the continuance of consciousness after death, in this
place where many have sought it, we have
abundant proof in other incontrovertible
Scriptures. The story of the rich man and ·
Lazarus clearly teaches that Lazarus (as well
as the rich man "in torment") was conscious
after he died and before the resurrection.*
The state of things depicted must be taken
as referring to the disembodied life this side
the resurrection, for the brothers of the rich
man were still alive upon the earth. At that
time, Lazarus was in Abraham's bosom, separated by an impassable gulf from the ungodly.
Poor consolation it had been for him to be in
Abraham's bosom, if he were unconscious, as
some would have it, and did not know that
he was there!

To the same effect are the never-to-be-for-

---

* Luke xvi. 19-31.

gotten words of Christ to the dying thief
upon the cross: "Verily, I say unto thee,
To-day thou shalt be with me in paradise!"*
What force could these words have, how
bring comfort to that dying sinner, if with
his expiring sigh he were to sink into a state
of dead unconsciousness, only to be broken
by the judgment-trumpet? What the meaning, on that supposition, of that word "To-
day"? To connect, as a few have ventured
to do, the word rendered "To-day," with the
words "I say unto thee"—"To-day I say
unto thee, etc.," is justly characterized by the
highest exegetical authority as "a violent
forcing of the sense of the passage."† "To-
day thou shalt be with me in paradise!"
Blessed words! well may we hold them fast.
They clearly teach that we shall not, in dying,
sink into a swoon of unconsciousness until
the judgment day. And they teach much
more than that, as we shall shortly see.

Paul teaches the same doctrine, once and
again. To the Corinthians ‡ he writes of the

---

* Luke xxiii. 43.

† See Meyer, "Commentary on Luke," *sub loc. cit.*

‡ 2 Cor. v. 1–4.

dissolution of "our earthly house of this tabernacle," and of a coming time wherein we shall be "unclothed." This unclothed state, he tells us, he did not regard as in itself desirable; for he adds, "We that are in this tabernacle do groan, being burdened; not for that we would be unclothed, but clothed upon." Nevertheless, he tells us, even thus, in view of death he was always "of good courage,"* because, so long as here "at home in the body," he was "absent from the Lord"; wherefore, he continues, "we are willing rather to be absent from the body, and to be at home with the Lord."

Similar is his language to the Philippians, in the near prospect of death. For we read, "What I shall choose, I wot not. For I am in a strait betwixt two, having a desire to depart and be with Christ, which is far better,"—† that is, of course, than life here. Surely such words as these of Paul to the Corinthians and the Philippians have no meaning except they imply that Paul expected to be conscious

---

* So the Revised version, *loc. cit.*

† Phil. i. 22, 24.

immediately after death, and while "absent from the body"! What possible satisfaction could there be in being unconsciously "at home with the Lord"?

To the same effect are the representations of the state of the departed saints which we find in the Apocalypse. Prior to the resurrection, according to all but some futurist interpreters, must we place the vision of the palm-bearing multitude standing before the throne. Are they unconscious? No, for John says that he heard them crying with a loud voice and saying, "Salvation to our God which sitteth upon the throne, and to the Lamb."* To the same effect is the whole glowing description of their condition and employment in the latter verses of the same chapter. They are "before the throne of God and serve Him day and night in His temple"; the Lamb feeds them and "leads them unto living fountains of waters." † Surely they are conscious!

The same remarks apply to the vision of the harpers upon the glassy sea.‡ They are

---

* Rev. vii. 10.   † *Ib.* vss. 15, 16.
‡ Rev. xv. 2–4.

described as a host of martyrs who have come victorious from the beast. The passage rep-resents their condition before the resurrection at the second advent, for the beast is not de-stroyed till the last of the vials is poured out, and this destruction is by the returning Lord. These heavenly harpers, therefore, at the time indicated in the vision, just before the out-pouring of the vials of wrath, are as yet in the disembodied state. Are they conscious or unconscious? Can any one doubt? For it is written that John in vision heard them singing "the song of Moses the servant of God, and the song of the Lamb"!

So also with the 144,000 with the Lamb on Mount Zion; they are also engaged in prais-ing God.* And even if any should so press the futurist interpretation of this book, as to insist that certainly in each of these cases we have representations of risen saints, still this could not be said of the passage which we find elsewhere, in which we read of the souls of martyrs whom John heard crying,—in words which show that their resurrection and

* Rev. xiv. 1-3.

reward had not yet come,—" How long, O Lord, holy and true, dost Thou not judge and avenge our blood upon them that dwell on the earth?"*

It is no answer to these testimonies to refer us to the symbolical character of the book. We admit that much even in the very visions to which we have referred must be symbolical. No one will insist that the palms and the harps and the white robes of these verses are literal, because in the case of disembodied souls, it is plain that these things must be taken in a figurative sense. But it is certain that a symbolical vision can not be made to teach, as these visions would otherwise teach, what is not merely different from, but actually contradictory of, the real state of the case. How is it conceivable that if the dead in Christ are really unconscious till the final judgment, as many will have it, that in these visions they should always have been represented as intensely conscious?

These Scriptures should be enough to settle the question. Against testimony so abun-

---

* Rev. v. 8.

dant and positive as that we have considered to urge that the application of the term "sleep" in the New Testament to the condition of the holy dead implies unconsciousness, can justly have but little force. For there are other reasons which in all ages, quite apart from any belief in the unconsciousness of the dead, have led men to speak of death as a sleep. There is, for instance, the outward resemblance of death to sleep. Like sleep, also, death brings cessation from the toils and the cares of life. And, again, in addition to these reasons, which might as well occur to a heathen, there is yet another which would give the adoption of the term "sleep" by the Spirit of God, a new fitness to denote death; namely, that even the body, for a time inactive in death as in sleep, is yet to be awakened as from sleep, at the last trumpet, then to take part for good or evil in an undying life.

Of as little weight are those Old Testament Scriptures which are often urged by those who maintain the sleep of the soul from death till resurrection. To examine each of such passages in detail would take us beyond the limits of this book. But we may well indicate

a consideration of which many seem to lose
sight in their use of Scripture passages in this
connection.   It should ever be remembered
that the affirmation of the plenary inspiration
of the Holy Scriptures does not carry with it
the affirmation of the truth of every statement
which we may find between the lids of the
Bible. The Bible is not a tabulated collection
of doctrinal statements; it is to a very large
extent a record of the sayings and doings of
living men, and, as we believe, an unerring
record.   But it is not inconsistent with their
inerrancy,—nay, their infallibility as such a
record even demands that when they give us
the sayings and beliefs of men who were bad
or ignorant, they shall state those beliefs as
they were held, and not as they were not held.

Thus, for example, it is true that we read
in the Book of Ecclesiastes, " the dead know
not anything"; "there is no knowledge nor
wisdom, in the grave whither thou goest"; *
and these words are often quoted to prove
that death is a state of unconsciousness.   But
such an application of the words shows that

---

* Eccl. ix. 5, 10.

the real character of the Book of Ecclesiastes is by those who make it forgotten or misapprehended. It is, we grant, inspired. We admit without reserve its infallibility. But it is inspired and infallible, *as a representation of that which it was intended to represent;* viz., the experience of a man seeking to gain satisfaction from the world.

Instead, therefore, of inspiration implying the infallible truth of each statement that we find in the book, the very fact that it is a record of this kind, compels us to say that a large part of its statements must be the opposite of true. They give, with unfailing exactness, the opinions and feelings of a worldly man of those days in regard to life and death, opinions which in the nature of the case must often have been wrong. And so the mere fact that one can adduce passages like that before us, from this book, proves nothing against the clear teachings of the New Testament, the direct words of Him who came and brought to light what was not with such clearness revealed before, namely, "life and immortality." Let one refuse to admit this, and he will be led to some startling conclusions

from this same book; as for instance, that "a man hath no pre-eminence above a beast"; *
and that "there is nothing better for a man than that he should eat and drink, and that he should make his soul enjoy good in his labor." †   There is, thus, no real antagonism between words such as these in Ecclesiastes and elsewhere, and the clear declarations of Christ and His apostles which teach or imply a consciousness after death.   We must in all cases distinguish between the opinions of men as contained in the Scripture record, from the teaching of that record itself.

A STATE OF REST.

THE Scriptures also teach that the state of the righteous between death and resurrection, is a state of rest.   In proof of this we should not cite, as some have done, the words of Job, "There the wicked cease from troubling, and there the weary be at rest." ‡
For although the book of Job is inspired, and is throughout a part of God's infallible word,

---

* Eccl. iii. 19.   † Eccl. ii. 24.   ‡ Job iii. 17

we are nowhere taught that Job himself was an inspired man. Very often, according to the teaching of the book of Job itself, Job spoke that which was not right, and his words on any subject, however they may be used to illustrate truth, can not be taken as in themselves proof of doctrine. That in this expression of his, however, Job was right, we learn elsewhere, even from the Old Testament.

In the book of Isaiah, it is the Lord who - uses by the prophet the following language: "The righteous perisheth and no man layeth it to heart. None considereth that the righteous is taken away from the evil (to come).* He shall enter into peace; they shall rest in their beds, each one that walketh in his uprightness." † These are plain statements. They tell us in so many words that "every one who walketh straight before him," ‡ his eye on the Lord and His kingdom, when he dies shall enter into peace, and in his bed of death shall find rest.

---

* The words "to come" have nothing corresponding to them in the Hebrew.

† Is. lvii. 1, 2 (R. V.)

‡ Delitzsch's rendering: see the Hebrew.

In the light of these words we are warranted
in understanding the idea of rest also to be
implied in all those New Testament passages
which refer to the death of believers as a sleep.
To the same effect are the words of the Spirit
in the Apocalypse, " Blessed are the dead that
die in the Lord from henceforth ; yea, saith
the Spirit, for they do rest from their labors." *
There is nothing regarding the departed people of God which, according to the Scripture,
we may say with more confidence than this,
that they have entered into rest.

In what does that rest consist? We may
answer, in the first place, with Isaiah,—In
rest from all "evil."   "The righteous is taken
away from the evil."   Death brings rest to
the believer from all that to him is evil.   He
shall have rest from all the outward cares and
sorrows of life.   The vexations and perplex-
ities of earthly business, the annoyances to
which we are subject in our social relations
will all end, with all such things, at death.

---

* Unless, possibly, with some expositors, we should
refer these words to the following vision, and understand them of the resurrection.

The believer will then have rest from the temptations and assaults of the evil one. How much this alone may signify, we probably can not know till at last we shall find ourselves for the first time in a place where Satan can not reach us. He is responsible for much more of our trouble than most people in these days give him credit for. So also will the believer have rest from the temptations and allurements of the world. Here we are in such relations with the world of sense, which is for the time now present under sin and Satan, that we can not possibly avoid the pressure of its influence, or escape wholly the force of its seductions.

> "The fondness of a creature's love—
> How strong it strikes the sense!
> Thither our strong affections move,
> Nor can we call them thence."

But with death the Christian, for the time, drops altogether out of this world of sense. From that time on he belongs to it no more, nor shall again till the day of "the regeneration"* or "restoration of all things,"† when,

---

* Matt. xix. 28.   † Acts iii. 21 (R. V.)

upon the reassumption of the body, he shall find the world of sense also " delivered," like himself and all believers, " from the bondage of corruption into the liberty of the glory of the children of God." *

So also shall the believer have rest in death from the warfare of the spirit against the flesh and the flesh against the spirit. No longer will he then have to say, " I see a law in my members warring against the law of my mind, and bringing me into captivity to the law of sin," † for the " members " are now laid aside, never again to be resumed as members of a weak and corruptible body, inciting to sin,— never more forever!

Then, often, the believer in this life is deeply saddened and wearied at heart by the prevalence of evil, of violence, and ungodliness, by the opposition, the ill-will, and misrepresentation of ungodly men. All this shall end with death. So also shall, for the saved, all pain and sorrow. For it is of the disembodied state before the resurrection that those words are used in the Apocalypse, " They

---

* Rom. viii. 21–23 (R. V.)   † Rom. vii. 23.

shall hunger no more, neither thirst any more; neither shall the sun strike upon them nor any heat : . . . . and God shall wipe away every tear from their eyes." * Hunger and thirst, and all that can cause pain and move to tears, shall end with death. From all these things we shall then have everlasting rest. All this, at least, must be comprehended in those words, " The righteous shall *rest* in their beds (of death); each one that walketh in his uprightness."

But is this all that is included in this promise of " rest " in the disembodied state? Not so, if we rightly understand the teaching of God's Word. For, keeping still that Word steadily before our eye, we must add, that from death till resurrection we shall rest from *labor.* For each servant of God, death will end work, till Jesus comes again. Not only will it end the work which is peculiar to life in this world in the body, but the intermediate state will be characterized by respite from every kind of active work for Christ.

As warrant for this statement, so contrary to

---

* Rev. vii. 16, 17 (R. V.)

3

the fancy of many, we have the direct declaration of our Lord, who said, with express ref erence to His approaching death: "We must work the works of Him that sent me while it is day; the night cometh, when no man can work." *   So also it is written by the apostle John, "Blessed are the dead that die in the Lord. . . . . Yea, saith the Spirit, for they do rest *from their labors;* and their works do follow them." †   The words used with regard to the last judgment are in harmony with this mode of representation.   For we read that believers are to give account in that day of "the things done *in the body.*" ‡   If our work for God continued in the disembodied state until the resurrection, can we suppose that such work should not come up also, as well as the work of this life, for estimation in the awards of the last day?

In perfect accord again with the same teaching is the fact that in all the representations which we have of the condition and occupations of the holy dead, they are never

---

* John ix. 4 (R. V.)   † Rev. xiv. 13.
‡ Greek, "*through* the body": see 2 Cor. v. 10.

represented as working still, in that disembodied life, for God. We do, indeed, read
that we shall judge the world, and shall judge
angels, with Christ ; * that God's servants shall
serve Him; † that one shall have authority
over two, another over ten cities,‡ and so on ;
and it is true that all these representations
and others like them do point forward to a
coming time when after death we shall enter
upon work for God. But on examination it
will be found that all such declarations are
distinctly referred in the Scriptures to the times
which shall be introduced by our Saviour's
second coming and the resurrection from the
dead. It is in the new earth, *after* the awards
of the great white throne, that God's servants
enter on those activities which are set forth
in Rev. xxi., xxii. ; it is after the Son of Man
comes to take account of His servants for the
things done in the body, that we first hear the
words, " Have thou authority over ten cities."
There is not one such passage which, looked
at in the light of other Scriptures, and espe-

---

* 1 Cor. vi. 2, 3.   † Rev. xxii. 3.

‡ Luke xix. 17–19.

cially of its own context, teaches that the intermediate state shall be a state of active work for God.

Still less can the words in Heb. i. be held to teach this, which we have heard cited in proof,—" Are they not all ministering spirits, sent forth to minister to those who shall be heirs of salvation?" *   So to use this passage is grossly to misapply Scripture. The words refer, as the context plainly shows us, to angels, and to angels only. To assume with some that death transforms men into angels, that is, into another order of beings, is as unscriptural as it is absurd. We are men here, and through whatsoever changes we may pass, we shall never become angels, but shall continue men forever.

We repeat then, that there is no exception to the fact that the Scriptures never once represent the holy dead as engaged in various higher labors for God, as many love to think, and as we are often even taught in funeral sermons. Such fancies belong, not to the theology of the holy Scriptures, but to that of

---

* Heb. i. 14.

the imagination   They are directly contradicted by the plain words of the Lord Jesus
Christ, who said that in the night of death " no
man can work."

The notions, therefore, which so many
fondly cherish of the ministrations of departed
friends, and even of intercourse with them,
however they may appeal to our desires and
affections, are totally without foundation in
the Word of God.   The bearing of this on
the pretences of modern spiritualism is self-
evident.

Yet let us not be misunderstood. For
while it is true that the Holy Word gives us
no ground for believing that the holy dead,
before the resurrection, are engaged in active
works for God, especially such as have to do
with this present world of sense, we must not -
infer that this implies a life of inactivity in
every sense of the word. For the same Word
which forbids us to think of the departed dead
as working for God, also represents them as,
in another way, intensely active.

The activity of the departed soul is, however, always represented as directed God-ward,
and not creature-ward.   In all the apocalyptic

representations of the intermediate state of
the blessed dead, they are shown to us as engaged in holy offices of worship and prayer.
Their service is therefore described as a temple service;* they are heard ascribing salvation to God and to the Lamb;† as join-
ing in that sublime ascription of praise and
thanksgiving, "Worthy is the Lamb that was
slain." ‡   They sing a new song which none
but they can learn.§   As the judgment angels
leave the heavenly sanctuary with the seven
last plagues to pour upon the earth, the blessed martyrs again are heard hymning "the song
of Moses the servant of God and the song of
the Lamb," saying, "Great and marvellous are
Thy works, O Lord God, the Almighty;
righteous and true are Thy ways, Thou King
of the ages"! ‖

Combining all these inspired representations
we are led to conclude that the disembodied
life will be, as compared with the present, a
life of rest from work.   The activities of the
soul in this present life are of necessity largely

---

* Rev. vii. 15.   † Rev. vii. 10.   ‡ Rev. v. 9–13.
§ Rev. xiv. 3.   ‖ Rev. xv. 2, 3 (R. V.)

turned toward the external, sensible world, and, according to the Scriptures, will after the resurrection again be so engaged, in a more exalted way. But in the intermediate state the activities of the soul appear from the Holy Word as exclusively turned God-ward. In other words, the present is a life marked predominantly by the outward, objective tendency. The sensible world claims and must needs have much of attention, insomuch that our service of God here for the most part must take the form of a service of men like ourselves in the flesh. But the life from death to resurrection will be herein in sharp contrast with the present. The world which he who is dead has left, still indeed exists, in matter and form, as he left it. Yet to him for the time being it is as if it were not. Though memory may go back to it, and perchance he who is gone may desire that he could again there work for the Master, yet work for him is now ended until resurrection come. In full accord with the Scriptures on this point are the following words of Martensen:

"The departed find themselves in a condition of rest, ... that they are in the night,

wherein no man can work.   Their kingdom is
not one of works and deeds, for they no longer
possess the conditions upon which works and
deeds are possible.   Nevertheless, they live a
deep spiritual life.   For the kingdom of the
dead is a kingdom of subjectivity, a kingdom
of calm thought and self-fathoming, a kingdom of *remembrance* in the full sense of the
word." *

Well worthy also of thought are the similar
words of Dorner, who, concerning the saints
in the world of the departed, has written as
follows:

"The life there is predominantly a life in
spirituality.   The essential, substantial union
of the soul with Christ still exists, nay, is
more untroubled and constant.   Through God
they are able to know about the world, and
learn to view everything in connection with
Christ.   In this world the realities of the
sensuous world are the objects of sight, the
spiritual world is the object of faith.   Then,
when the physical side is wanting to the spirit,
these poles will be reversed.   To the de-

---

* "Christian Dogmatics," § 276, p. 458.

parted spirits, the spiritual world, whether in good or evil, will appear to be the real existence resting on immediate evidence." *

All these particulars, then, and especially this last—too often overlooked or denied in our thoughts and words about the future,—are taught us in the Scripture as included in the conception of the " rest " into which the believer enters at death, and the state in which he shall abide until the resurrection.

WITH CHRIST.

ANOTHER feature characteristic of the intermediate state of the blessed dead, according to the uniform and clearest representations of the Holy Scriptures, will be this, that, as contrasted with the present, it will be a state wherein we shall be with Christ. So our blessed Lord, when on the cross, told the dying thief, " To-day thou shalt be with me in Paradise." † Such also was Paul's expectation. He tells us plainly that for the believer

---

* "System of Christian Doctrine," § 153, iii. 3.
† Luke xxiii. 43.

to be "absent from the body," was to be "at home with the Lord." *   Not in the mere fact of being delivered from a life in the body, as we have already seen, did Paul rejoice in the prospect of death. On the contrary, he speaks of that sundering of soul from body as in itself, to him—as to us—undesirable. And yet he could rejoice even in the expectation of this temporary disembodiment, because of this overwhelming and most blessed compensation, that in that state he should find himself "at home with the Lord."

And so much did this thought fill his mind when contemplating this state to which death would introduce him, that he tells us again, that, looking, on the one hand, at the work for Christ which he was doing here, and so loved to do, and which must stop for him at death, and then thinking, on the other hand, of the beatific presence of Christ into which the very article of death would introduce him, he was "in a strait betwixt the two, having the desire to depart and to be with Christ"; because this was "very far better." †

---

* 2 Cor. v. 8 (R. V.)   † Phil. i. 23 (R. V.)

How much this alone will signify, those will best understand who best love Christ. To be with Christ! with Him, the incarnate Son of God, most blessed and most holy! Him, who for love of us died upon the cross, and who, now glorified, is in the full possession of that glory which He had with the Father before the world was!*—to behold Him in His glory and be with Him—what must it be! If that brief transfiguration vision of Jesus glorified, even as mortal eyes were able to behold Him, was such as to cause Peter to exclaim, "Lord! it is good for us to be here!" what shall it be, to be with the glorified Lord in Paradise!

A SINLESS STATE.

TO what has been said the Scriptures authorize us to add this also, that in the intermediate state the believer will be perfectly freed from sin. For this immeasurable blessing, he will not have to wait till resurrection. And yet, most strange to say, this has

---

* John xvii. 24.

been doubted or denied of late by eminent
evangelical theologians, as Dorner, Martensen,
and others. Dorner, for example, argues as
follows:

" If believers are conceived as holy immediately after death, sanctification would be
effected by the separation from the body ; the
seat, therefore, of evil must be found in the
body, and sanctification would be realized
through a mere suffering, namely, of death;
in a physical process, instead of through the
will." *   To suppose that God might sanctify
by a creative sanctifying act, the soul in the
very article of death, were, in his opinion,
" to abridge the ethical sphere and its laws,"
and would imply "a violation of the fundamental law obtaining in the relation between
divine and human agency." †

But these considerations, however plausible
they may appear to some, do not for us suffice
to set aside the common faith of the Protestant Churches that, for a regenerated man, to
die is to be freed from sin. We believe that

---

* " System of Christian Doctrine," § 153, iii. 2.
† *Ib.*

"the souls of believers are at their death made perfect in holiness." It is true that the declarations of the New Testament upon this subject are not so numerous and dogmatic in form as might, perhaps, have been expected. And yet we can hardly be wrong in recalling here the words in the Epistle to the Hebrews, where we read of "the general assembly and church of the first-born, ... and the spirits of just men made perfect." * For while the word rendered "made perfect" might in itself conceivably refer only to that legal perfecting of which we read elsewhere in this epistle, yet we have to read these words in the light of their context and of other passages, which, if they do not directly affirm, yet give the strongest reason for affirming that for those who are saved, to depart this life is to be made perfect in holiness. The apostle John tells us that to see Christ as He is, will have the effect of making us like Him.† But we are elsewhere told that we shall be with Christ immediately after death, and shall, therefore, then see Him as He is. Is not the conclusion irresistible that then we shall be like Him?

---

* Heb. xii. 23. † 1 John iii. 2.

The same may be inferred from the words already quoted from the Apocalypse regarding the departed dead,—" They shall hunger no more, neither thirst any more." * Surely these words in their connection can hardly be supposed to refer merely to the cessation of bodily hunger and thirst. They must needs have the spiritual meaning which the whole context requires. They send us for the key to their meaning to that beatitude pronounced by our Lord when on the earth,— " Blessed are they which do hunger and thirst after righteousness ; for they shall be filled."†

As for the objections urged by Dorner and others, we answer, in the first place, that although separation of the soul from the body brings perfect and immediate separation from sin, yet it by no means follows that the seat of sin must be the body. For while it is true that sin, in many instances, is due to causes that lie in our physical nature, and that with the absence of this body such incitements and occasions of sin will cease, yet these are not all the occasions of sin which come to the

---

* Rev. vii. 16.　　　　　† Matt. v. 6.

regenerated man. Many others are found in the conditions of this present earthly life.

The world in which we live, and of which we form, in the moral sense, a part, is itself, through the influences of a society made up of unconverted and but imperfectly sanctified men, as mighty, perhaps, as the body, to seduce the believer into sin. Nor must we forget, again, that we are living in a world which, for the present age, is characterized by the presence and active power of the devil, no small part of whose working, as we are repeatedly told in the Scriptures, is in order to lead the people of God into sin.

Death is thus not to be conceived of as merely a sundering of the relation of soul and body. Because it is that, it is much more than that. It also removes a Christian from all these other provocatives to sin which come from outside the body. Not by any means, therefore, does the doctrine of perfect sanctification at death imply that sin must be occasioned in the believer by the body only. Rather should we put the matter in this way. If a man is truly regenerate, then his will, even here, as to its prevailing bent and habit is not for sin, but against it. It is, however, a weak will. It is also often misled by imperfect knowledge, so that the man often sins without knowing at the time that he is sinning. Under these conditions, when tempted by bodily infirmity, or the pressure of social influence, or more mysteriously by Satan, or perchance by all together, it is not strange that even though in regeneration the will is unalterably set for God, it should often unknowingly, or even knowingly, consent to sin.

Suppose, however, not only the body, but all these external temptations and occasions to sin to be removed, as we know that they will be removed by death; then let us remember the immense addition to our knowledge which the very fact of death must bring with it; and, above all, the immediate and unbroken communion with Christ to which death will introduce us: and is it not then easy to see how sanctification may be perfected at death even by "a truly ethical process"?

But, in the last place, if any one feel a difficulty still remaining, surely we may postulate, if anything more be needed, the mighty power of Christ as sufficient in any case to give at once that perfect holiness for which the believer longs. Nor would this violate any law regulating the relation between divine and human action. Dorner's objection to this effect proceeds upon the assumption that God can not make any course of moral action certain in a free agent without destroying thereby his freedom. But this assumption is contradicted both by Scripture and by experience. Many acts are certain before they occur, and yet are free. It would even make salvation impossible as a *certain* thing; for what is the final salvation but the attainment of an assured certainty that the man will sin no more? Was it uncertain when God undertook in Christ for sinners, whether such a result would be attained or no?

Moreover the Scriptures always refer the regeneration of a sinner, not to his own free act, but to the mighty power of God. But if God can thus regenerate a man without destroying or restricting his free agency, then surely faith need have no trouble in believing that the same power which regenerated is quite able to effect that perfect sanctification at death for which we long, and which the Scrip-

tures lead us to expect.   Nor need we fear,
with Dorner, lest thereby the moral quality of
a holiness thus attained should be destroyed,
or any law regarding the relation between
divine and human action should thereby be
violated.

A STATE OF PREPARATION.

BUT while we understand the Word of
God as teaching that "the souls of
believers are at their death made perfect in
holiness," we are not, therefore, to understand
this as implying that there will therefore after
death be no further room for growth in holiness.   The perfection in holiness which we
shall then have, will be a perfection in *quality*,
but *not* in *degree*.   It implies the total absence
of sin and defilement, while yet it remains
none the less possible — let us rather say,
necessary,—that all the elements of a holy
character shall continue to grow and gather
strength, not only during the intermediate
state, but forever and forever.

And so, from the point of view which we
have now reached, the intermediate state ap-

pears as a state of special training and disci-
pline for the high service of that kingdom
which is to be revealed at the second appearing of the Lord. Such a conception, indeed,
seems to follow of necessity from the very
laws of the soul's being. For it is in the very
nature of the soul that it must needs grow,
whether in good or evil. For it to stand still
in either regard, is impossible. That is true
even now and here. But after death we shall
be, according to God's promise, placed under
conditions more favorable for growth than
here. Here, so to speak, we are kept, not
under the immediate instruction of Christ,
but "under tutors and governors till the time
appointed of the Father." But then, in a
sense which is not true now, we shall be
"with Christ"; we shall be taken out from
under the "tutors and governors" which train
us here, and brought under the immediate
tuition of Him who spake as never man spake;
and then and thus we shall have entered the
last and highest class in the school of prepa-
ration for Christ's kingdom.

Can any one doubt the result of this?
Growth in holiness here is measured by the

constancy and intimacy of the soul's communion with Christ. What, then, will the growth be when we shall spend the blessed, peaceful, holy years until the resurrection day, in fellowship, immediate and unbroken by any distraction, with the Lord himself! Is it not clear that we must then think of the intermediate state, as, in an eminent degree, a state of further training, education, and progress toward that exalted spiritual power and perfection which we shall need when at last, with the return of the Lord to earth, the time comes for us to be made rulers over many things, according to His promise?*

A STATE OF IMPERFECTION.

FROM all this it follows that the intermediate state, while a state of freedom from sin and pain, and of immediate fellowship with Christ, is yet a state, in other respects, of imperfection. This imperfection consists, firstly, in this, that it is a life without the body. So long as this bodiless

* Matt. xxv. 21, 23.

condition lasts, the soul has, so far as we know, no organ by which it can communicate with the visible and external world. Thus its activities, as we have already seen, are, during the intermediate state, restricted. Of this proof has been already given, and need not be repeated.

The imperfection of the intermediate state appears further from the fact that not at death, nor at any time during the continuance of this dispensation, is the promised reward given to God's people. Thus, we are told regarding the saints of the old dispensation, that they "all died in faith, not having received the promises, ... God having provided some better thing for us, that they, without us, should not be made perfect."* Herein the imperfection, in certain respects, of the departed saints, is declared in so many words. All the saints are to be perfected at the same time.

To the same effect are all the numerous representations of the New Testament, wherein the second coming of the Lord to earth,

---

* Heb. xii. 13, 49.

and never the death of the individual believer,
is set forth as the time for the distribution of
the rewards for the labors and self denials of
this life.   Thus Paul, writing just before his
martyrdom, tells us that from henceforth there
was laid up for him " a crown of righteousness
which the Lord, the righteous Judge," should
give him " at that day," and not to him only,
but "to all them also that love His appearing."*   Not yet, then, has Paul received his
crown.   " That day " has not yet come.   For
the crowning day, Paul, with all the saints in
Paradise, is waiting still.

So also our Lord gives us the same teaching in the parables of the talents and of the
pounds.†   In the latter of these He teaches us
in so many words, that it was "after a long
time " that the Lord of those servants came
and reckoned with them ; and that they received their reward, not one by one, but all
together when the Lord returned, " having
received the kingdom."   So also, on another
occasion, He said of those who, when they

---

* 2 Tim. iv. 8.

† Matt. xxv. 14–30.   Luke xix. 12–27.

made a feast, called thereto the poor and needy, that they should be recompensed "at the resurrection of the just." *

To this mode of representation there is absolutely no exception. In not a solitary case does the Scripture connect the bestowal of the promised "reward" with the believer's death. Whatever he receives of blessing at death in addition to what he has now, can only still be regarded as an "earnest" of good things to come.

Hence it follows that a very common mode of speaking on this subject ought, according to the Word, to be rejected. How often are we told at funerals and on other occasions, even by the authorized expounders of the Word of God, that the departed "has now received his reward," and so on, whereas this mode of speaking is not only without warrant in the Scripture, but is directly contrary to its plain teachings. It is indeed of kin to that modern type of exegesis which makes the coming of the Son of Man to this world to signify the going of departing souls to Him!

---

* Luke xiv. 12–14.

Surely we shall do wisely to conform our mode
of speaking on this subject,—one concerning which we can know nothing at all, except
what God has told us,—to the teaching of our
Lord and His apostles. The prevailing mode
of representation—or rather, misrepresentation,—has already done quite enough to turn
away the mind of the Church from that glori-
ous appearing of the Lord for resurrection,
which the New Testament holds before us as
the one great Hope of the Church, to fix it
instead on the death of the individual believer as the ultimatum of Christian hope!
Let us remember, then, that the intermediate
state of believers, while, according to the
Scriptures, "far better" than the present, is
also, according to the same inspired authority,
in the respects indicated, a state of imperfection.

A STATE OF FAITH AND HOPE.

IF this is so, then it follows, lastly, that
the disembodied life will, like the present, be a life wherein there will be place for
faith and hope. It is true that much which

we now know only by faith, will then be matter of personal experience and immedi- ate vision. But still, until it shall please the Lord to command the resurrection of the body, and therewith to bestow upon all His people their destined rewards, there will still remain abundant·room for the exercise of faith, and hope, and patience.

This receives a touching illustration from the scene in the Apocalypse where the souls of the martyrs are heard crying, "How long, O Lord, holy and true, dost Thou not judge and avenge our blood on them that dwell on the earth?" And to this holy longing after the full triumph of the kingdom of God on earth, we read that "it was answered that they should rest yet for a time, till their fel- low servants also, and their brethren, that should be killed as they were, should be ful- filled."*

And so it appears, as the result of our in- quiry, that the truth of God's holy Word in regard to the state of the righteous dead lies at an equal remove from two erroneous extremes:

* Rev. vi. 10, 11.

namely, from the Romish doctrine of a purgatory, through which the most even of true
Christians must pass, that through its cleans-
ing fires they may be fitted for the heavenly
life; and, no less, from the popular modern
Protestant view, which refuses to admit any
practical distinction as to perfection, enjoy-
ment, and reward, between the intermediate
and the resurrection state beyond.

As for the doctrine of purgatory, it is utter-
ly without foundation in God's Word; and
few doctrines have brought forth worse fruit
in the practical life of the Church. A mere
reference to the days of Tetzel, Luther, and
the great Reformation, not to speak of the
present, is sufficient to illustrate this.

As for the other extreme, which makes the
believer's redemption and reward practically
complete at death, it is as totally unscriptural
as the doctrine of purgatory. It has, moreover, done very much to divert the mind of
Christians from that personal return of the
Lord Jesus, for which He has commanded us
all to watch and wait. It has thus greatly
changed the type of Christian thought and
character from that which Christ has set before

us as a model in His Word. It has also tended
to modify doctrinal belief on matters upon
which the Bible lays much stress. For by thus
exaggerating the glory and perfection of the
intermediate state, it has come to pass that, to
the minds of many, the second advent of our
Lord and the judgment are made to seem a
superfluity. No logical place is left for such
an event in their theology. Hence soon appears indifference to the Church's Hope, often
to be followed,—as, alas, frequent experience
of late has shown,—by the outright denial of
this fundamental article of Christian faith.
Let us therefore beware of this error, and
hold fast to the Word of God!

Blessed indeed are the dead that die in
the Lord!—blessed from the instant of death!
They do rest from their labors. Tears are
wiped away from their eyes, and in holy ad-
oration they serve God day and night in His
temple. Yet, blessed as they are, they are
still looking forward—as we also should be—
to a day which shall be more blessed still! the
day of all days, the day of the return of the
Lord Jesus to the earth* in the glory of His

---

* Acts i. 11.

kingdom ; the Hope of the whole undivided
Church in heaven and on earth,* the day of
the bridal of the Lamb,† the full triumph of
the kingdom of God,‡ and the everlasting re-
newal of the old, sin-burdened creation. "For
the whole creation groaneth and travaileth in
pain together until now, waiting for the adoption, to wit, the redemption of the body."§
"Amen. Even so. Come, Lord Jesus."
Amen and Amen.

WHERE ?

AND so the Church which is with Christ is
awaiting her return to earth with Him !
And where? How often the question is asked !
Yet we can only answer it by saying that
nothing is clearly revealed. " In Paradise ? "
Yes ! truly ! But then where is " Paradise " ?
Who can tell us this ? We know, indeed,
that the holy dead are "with Christ." But
who can tell us how much we are to put into

---

* 1 Thess. i. 10; 1 Tim. i. 1.   † Rev. xix. 7–9.
‡ Rev. xi. 15; *cf.* vv. 17, 18; xix. 6.
§ Rom. viii. 23, and context.

this phrase? Does it give us the right to affirm that the spirits of the just are in that particular portion of space which at present retains the glorified humanity of our Lord? Perhaps so; yet we dare not dogmatize here. We cannot but remember that we are wholly unable to define with precision the relations of disembodied spirit to space. Most suggestive, to our mind, are the following words of Martensen:

"If it be asked where those who are fallen asleep find themselves after death,—nothing can be more preposterous than the idea that they are separated from us by an outward infinity, that they find themselves in some other material world, etc. By such notions we retain the departed within those limits and conditions of sense beyond which they certainly are. No barrier of sense separates them from us, for the sphere in which they find themselves differs in every respect from this material sphere of time and space. As we may figuratively say regarding the man who is asleep and dreaming, though he is not separated outwardly and locally from the material

world around him, yet that he is relatively beyond or above the world, and 'absent' or
departed from it, ... the same may be said
in an absolute sense of those who have departed this life. . . . . Instead of the modern
notion that the soul wings its way to the stars,
which is sometimes understood literally, as if
the soul were borne to another actual world,
the idea is far more correct that it draws itself back into the innermost and mystical
chambers of existence which underlie the outward. . . . . A realm *beneath* or *under* is the
cosmical description which revelation gives us
of Hades. . . . . The realm of the dead, in
relation to this world of sense, must be called
the *deeper* region."*

But however this may be, as to the place
or the manner of the life from death till resurrection, we need concern ourselves but little.
It is written, " Say ye unto the righteous, It
shall be well with him." Even that were
enough. And so, with the eye of faith fixed
on the atoning, reigning, and returning Lord,

------

* " Christian Dogmatics," § 276, pp. 459, 460.

we may well trustfully say with one of the sweet singers of the Church:

> " My knowledge of that life is small;
> The eye of faith is dim ;
> But 'tis enough that Christ knows all,
> And I shall be *with Him !* "

www.ingramcontent.com/pod-product-compliance
Lightning Source LLC
Chambersburg PA
CBHW021516090426
42739CB00007B/646